BETTER IMPLEMENTATION NOW!

Eight Ways Great Strategies Fail & How To Fix Them

Theresa Ashby, MBA, PhD

INDIE BOOKS
INTERNATIONAL

ISBN-10: 1-947480-55-3
ISBN-13: 978-1-947480-55-1
Library of Congress Control Number: 2019938155

Operational Action Response Teams® (OART) is a registered trademark of Theresa Ashby

Designed by Joni McPherson, mcphersongraphics.com

INDIE BOOKS INTERNATIONAL, LLC
2424 VISTA WAY, SUITE 316
OCEANSIDE, CA 92054

www.indiebooksintl.com

CONTENTS

PART I

Why Great Strategies Are Not Enough

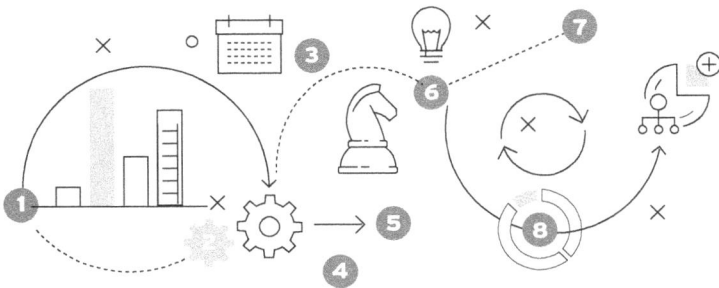

CHAPTER 1

•••

Why Even Great Strategies Fail

Lack of implementation planning is the enemy of all great strategies.

When Joseph, the first nonfamily CEO of a medical device company, had to recall millions of dollars' worth of a product, he became apoplectic. It thrust the organization into a downward spiral of financial decline. It was as though a frozen lake cracked underneath his feet and he dropped into the ice-cold water—systemically, something was amiss. He was compelled to analyze the entire strategy for the survival of the organization.

Chances are, if you have been in an executive position or are an entrepreneur, you have experienced a challenge that caused you to ask yourself, "What went wrong?"

Before this incident, Joseph would have continued to have faith in the strategy the organization had created, thinking it would be enough to drive the organization on an upward trajectory. After the desperate reanalysis, however, he agreed the strategy was still correct but admitted there had been no implementation planning—there was a lack of connection to the organizational culture, no plans to change operations accordingly, and unprepared leaders without requisite skills. He found employees unwilling to execute—it was too much work. Systems and processes were misaligned, causing barriers that hindered the company's ability to meet expectations and projected profits. There were no strategic champions—just many people trying to act strategically at the cost of operational tactics.

Michael Porter, in the 1980s, was dubbed the "father of strategy." As a university professor at Harvard Business School, he created some of the most influential models on the subject of strategy. Because of his work, the business community grew to understand and accept his definition of strategy, and it is still the basis of all strategy work. Since then, however, others have created new ideas and concepts about strategy, integrating our new economic landscape.

Recently, and because of so many stories like Joseph's, professionals and scholars have turned their attention to figuring out why seemingly perfect strategies fail to produce sufficient ROI (return on investment) across the organization's ecosystem. Researchers project that failure rates for strategic implementation are anywhere from 60 percent to 80 percent; some state even higher figures.

A survey[1] of more than 400 global CEOs from Asia, Europe, and the United States found that execution of company strategy was the number one challenge. Among the other challenges listed were innovation, geopolitical instability, and top-line growth—and none of these are going away anytime soon.

Economic Sustainability

Every new day brings a new set of issues and opportunities for every CEO, manager, and entrepreneur in the world. The leader's commitment must be to continue the vitality of the organization—to drive our economy. The success of a company goes beyond the confines of its four walls (for some companies, the four walls are metaphorical). There is an economic circle of life when a company is doing well. People are more satisfied if their work is purposeful; more money is inserted into the economy, and a vast number of new opportunities can emerge when things are working well. One should admire leaders and entrepreneurs who build empires that help create economic sustainability.

Leaders should have an economic mindset, a powerful sense of responsibility for all of their employees, customers, and vendors—an understanding and contemplation over creating the best possible products and services without compromise.

[1] Sull, Donald, Rebecca Homkes, and Charles Sull. "Why Strategy Execution Unravels—and What to Do About It." *Harvard Business Review*, March 2015.

Predictability of Growth

As businesses grow, their strategies, objectives, and priorities shift according to the business lifecycle. Each stage brings with it its own predictable set of growth opportunities and barriers. An appreciation of the lifecycle stages leads to a better understanding of how one builds a strategy, thus developing a more robust implementation plan that better aligns with the reality of organizational constraints.

A note here before I outline the five stages of the business lifecycle: this book is especially helpful for the growth, expansion, and maturity stages. The seed and start-up phases need their own strategic discourse and are not addressed in this book, but are worthy of at least a mention.

Seed Stage. This is the beginning. You have ideas, and you seek advice and opinions of others including potential clients, industry experts, market research, etc. This is the stage in which you consider the feasibility of the business idea, the financial foundation, and viability—it is a go or no-go decision.

Start-Up Stage. It is a go. You spend time developing and refining the product or service and gathering feedback from early adopters. This stage can bring on a lot of confusion and requires adaptability and flexibility. Cash flow, or lack of it, will be a constant battle. But a few years down the road, there will be enough customers to thrust you into growth.

Growth Stage. At this stage, the business should be gaining new customers and consistent income. Cash flow should begin to improve, and potentially, new ideas for the company are generated. In preparation for this stage, many systems and processes should be established, and ways to improve should be sought. Here the leader must be sensible about dividing time among managing increased revenues, customer needs, new deals, competition, and accommodating an expanding workforce while simultaneously balancing time on the front lines. There is no time like the present to build a strategic implementation plan. This plan will keep everyone on target and task. Without a plan, in this stage, chaos can ensue, and everyone will be dancing to a different tune.

Expansion Stage. Capitalizing on the stability of this stage offers an opportunity to expand a business into new products, services, or markets. There is rapid growth in both revenue and cash flow, but you should not become complacent. Hypervigilance is always wise—become too comfortable, and a competitor can take over your market share, or employees can take the organization in a completely different direction than the leader intended. Leaders must always be looking forward with a desire to expand; otherwise, a decline will surely happen. On the flip side, expansion should be well thought out, and risk factors well defined—expanding too rapidly can significantly risk the viability of the organization.

This is where a strategic implementation plan becomes so critical. It can address the resources and realistically identify the impact of time, cost, and ROI.

Questions to be asked at this stage include: Is the organization fit to expand? If so, who will lead the charge? What is the best method of expansion? Where should we expand? When should we expand? Why is it important to expand this particular product, service, or into this market? How are we going to prepare the organization for expansion?

By answering these questions, the execution of a company strategy becomes more likely.

Maturity Stage. This is the most stable stage and also carries the most risk for decline. Do you remember Blockbuster Video? There are several choices at this stage: Figure out how to reinvent, expand, or exit the business. Leaders must create a balance between becoming an organizational dinosaur and living in a constant world of change. There is a prime balance.

Not all businesses go through all of the stages. In fact, it is estimated that 25 percent of all businesses never make it out of the start-up stage.

This review of the lifecycle is intended to simply help you navigate your way into building a strategic plan that can be implemented successfully.

Real Work

Someone once said successful companies work on processes versus projects. How often have you heard someone say, "They all seem so busy, but I feel like no work is getting done"? What is really happening is work is getting done, just not the *real* work that is needed to move the strategy forward.

An executive client once shared that despite working ten-hour days, there was always more work on his desk. And yet, when his annual review came in from the board of directors, it contained low marks for meeting strategic objectives. There was a huge misalignment between what the board thought was "real work" and what the executive thought was "real work." This all changed when the executive created a matrix that showed the work being done in comparison to the strategic objectives— many items were removed from his tasks and new, more directed tasks were added. When he went back to the board with the matrix, they increased his marks. He then cascaded the matrix throughout the organization to help align all work objectives.

Strategic Mindset

A strategic mindset is how everyone thinks throughout the organization—it is a thought process that everything one does it must advance the strategy.

As a mindset, and despite the many differences in organizations, many companies that achieve sustainable growth share a common set of beliefs, attitudes, values, and behaviors. Thus, they allow employees to share a common language so objectives can move forward productively in alignment with the strategy.

It is also true that companies obsessed with a clear vision, mission, and values turn their focus on execution of the strategy—building core competitive advantage over other companies in the same industry.

A quick note: In the chapters ahead, I will not be outlining a program for businesses to *develop* their strategy. The assumption is that the strategy from which you are working is a great strategy. Strategic development is a process about which much has been written, and it is not the scope of this book. My goal here is instead to identify practical ideas for achieving an implementation plan that is sustainable over time and can lead to better results in a much shorter time frame, with more profit and more engagement.

CHAPTER 2

••

Eight Ways Great Strategies Fail

I wish there were a simple way of developing and implementing strategy. But the reality is organizations are a complicated ecosystem of moving segments—some predictable and others not. Developing and implementing a strategy can make you feel like you are balancing on a tightrope twenty-five stories above the Earth trying to run to get from one narrow platform to the next—without a safety net.

Executives are charged with successfully balancing people, profits, and process with a ruthless focus on the outcomes and priorities devised in the strategy. They must set aside their egos for the greater good and require everyone to live up to the highest standards to quickly accomplish all of the tasks at hand.

There are eight ways great strategies fail and ways to fix those failures:

- **Not connecting mission to strategy.** A common mistake is not taking an organization's mission, vision, values, and culture—defined by the question, what is the organization's reason for being?—into account when planning strategy. The answer to that question needs to be the guiding star to navigate the strategy. Align all strategic decisions with the mission. Fix: Connect mission, vision, values, and culture to strategy.

- **Pushing strategies down from the top.** This failure occurs when executives do not involve their people during all phases of the strategic planning process. Don't create strategy in isolation and expect people to be fully engaged in its execution. Talk to people in a variety of areas to gather ideas and a true understanding of what is really going on. Fix: Pull input from the bottom up.

- **Not understanding the real meaning of strategy.** People get confused about the difference between the layers of strategy and the requirements for execution. The first step is to understand and define the types of strategies and what role one plays in execution. Fix: Teach the real meaning of strategy.

- **Neglecting the critical few.** Sometimes too many people think they are strategic, and that leads to not enough people doing the work. Not everyone needs to be a strategic thinker. There is a vital need for people to perform tactical implementation in the most productive manner possible. Fix: Concentrate on the critical few.

- **Failure to maintain focused momentum.** This failure happens when nobody really knows what role they play in the implementation plan. The result is nothing gets fully accomplished. The top needs to help focus various groups on their critical role in the implementation of the strategy. Fix: Maintain focused momentum.

- **Squandering the resources.** Often, great strategic ideas fail for lack of dedicated resources. Sometimes necessary resources are being wasted on lower priority projects. The top must find adequate resources to accomplish strategic objectives. Strategy requires that the organization say "No" to the good so it can say "Yes" to the great. Fix: Align limited resources to critical priorities.

- **Misaligning function and flow.** Sometimes projects and objectives are allowed to proceed which are actually at odds with the desired strategy. The top must be ruthless in aligning the function and flow of strategic implementation. Allowing pet projects to continue is a luxury that today's organization cannot afford. Fix: Align function and flow.

- **Not properly preparing the executive team.** Never assume an executive team knows how to implement strategy or is dedicated to it. Correct strategic implementation is an acquired skill. Invest in developing the proper mindset for executives to set the organization up for success and equip them with the tools. Fix: Prepare the executive.

The Setup

Let us be honest, shall we? We all work hard to create the best possible strategy. Often in an effort to have a great plan, we work fast on the development in isolation. Company leaders have been doing the same thing for decades—and yet, all of the brilliant plans created at strategic planning retreats have failed rather miserably when it came to implementation, and they continue to fail at an estimated rate of between 50 percent to 90 percent. I am dedicated to changing these statistics and that is why I am writing this book—in hopes that we all get better at the implementation—to run more successful business and enjoy life. Further more, if you believe, as I do, business is the only thing driving our economy, then these percentages are unacceptable.

Perhaps you are asking yourself, who said that about the "brilliant plans," and why is there such a significant gap in the quoted percentages? The actual number is difficult to measure because the precise number of failures in both public and private companies is unlikely to be accurately recorded. And if truth were told, who wants to admit to the public they failed.

The most important area for us to examine, then is how to get better at the process of executing strategy. What if we ran our businesses with the intention of an 85 percent implementation success, changing the failure rate to only 15 percent? At least that would be better than 50 percent. But of course, we would rather reduce our failure rate to zero.

The airline industry runs its business with the intent to be hundred percent accurate for all flights arriving safely to their destination—can you imagine if they said we have a tolerance for a 1 percent failure rate? Let us take a look at some data on commercial air travel from the Aviation Safety Network Worldwide (ASNW): in 2017 there were 36.8 M flights across the globe and 59 fatalities. According to data from the ASNW accident rate now stands at one fatal passenger accident per 7,360,000 flights. If the airlines were to stop improving and accept one percent failure rate for all flights than 368,000 thousand people would die each year. Who would ever get on a plane? The entire commercial flight industry would collapse. Both loss of life and collapse of an industry is just not acceptable.

What failure rate can your organization withstand? There are many industries that have a life and death proposition if something goes wrong. For others, it is the survival of the organizations and the livelihoods of people we employ. This is why it is so important to continue working to reduce the failure rate of businesses. Let's talk specifics about the development of strategy.

Strategy has become a *thing* now—and it is the thing we do. Every year, whether it is necessary or not, strategy sessions are scheduled and overly optimistic agendas are constructed for the upcoming year. Executives may find themselves sequestered in a dark, dingy conference room, or for some, at a golf retreat experience. These business retreats can last anywhere from half a day to a five-day period, with group activities scheduled in between. The strategy-building activities are intended to create a more cohesive way of working together and should—if things go perfectly—result in a *brilliant plan* for the organization's year ahead.

Since executives are focused strictly on strategy, their activities are aimed at achieving that one goal, not team-building. That pursuit should be split off into a separate conference session. It is a waste of valuable time and energy if the event tries to cover too many areas of interest instead of the specific strategic task. It will also dilute the message and the energy needed to develop a sound strategy. I participated in a three-day strategic retreat that was announced as such by the CEO. When we arrived, we were all handed the results of an executive team survey we had filled out months earlier. The CEO announced, "I decided to share the team results before we move into creating our new strategy." As he began to hand out results, vocal rumbling exploded. No one came emotionally prepared to be critically analyzed and discuss the results, and by the way, the results regarding how we all worked together were horrific. There went any opportunity to be collaborative and willing to negotiate changes over the next two-and-one-half days.

Once completed, strategic plans formulated at such retreats will either be foisted onto those further down the corporate ladder to decode and work through or (even worse) the results of the weekend's work may be scrapped altogether so the CEO can put together the plan he intended to implement in the first place.

Preparing for the strategic planning session, then, can be a significant waste of time, money, and resources that all end up squandered. Weeks or even months might be spent making these often-futile preparations. Gathering information, planning the agenda, putting the PowerPoint(s) together, figuring out the perfect mix of activities, and figuring out the logistics can be a nightmarish set of tasks if the result is little to no positive movement.

When it is time for all of the executives (some vice presidents or equivalents), perhaps a facilitator and a note-taker to assemble and begin the work of building the proposed plan, the attitudes of those in attendance are often quite disparate. Some may be excited about the opportunity to be heard, some are hopeful, and others still may exhibit anger at the idea of making any sort of changes.

Have you ever overheard someone say, "Well, I hope this time it will be different," or, "I would rather be spending time with my family?" The most likely interpretation comes down to, "Argh! I do not have time for this, and I need to be back at the office," or "I don't care about this nonsense, and these people don't know anything about what we do. I'm just going to continue to do what I want to in my own department." Yes, we might want to go to a resort-style retreat location and hit a round or two of golf with our business colleagues. But the truth is, most people would rather go to such a place with close friends or family and enjoy the outing in a more relaxed and less pressured way (although for some, the company is the *family* company).

Any of these mental models are difficult to change.

In between the fun activities that are meant to be a break from the serious proceedings, lengthy periods of discussions will fill up the days of work and planning. The *who*, *what*, *when*, *where*, and *how* of growing the business through new or existing assets, increased capabilities, increased market share, and talent management will all be endlessly debated. These conversations will be supported by information gathered from spreadsheets, history, opinions, and the experiences of others. Competition for funding is likely to arise as each department advocate attempts to protect the status quo via budgets, staffing, and perceived position. Unfortunately, there may also be an attitude of scarcity on display as egos take control.

The ideal state to aspire to for effective and productive meetings is an atmosphere where egos are kept in check; leaders are willing to both give and receive, information is shared generously, and there is an overall attitude of abundance.

Effective strategic planning involves making decisions that either cut off possibilities and options or identify possibilities and options. The executives who are involved in strategic planning may feel fearful that getting those decisions wrong will wreck their careers—and that can be an uneasy sensation for anyone. But well-planned strategies include risks, a level of openness to a less-than-perfect plan, and incorporate flexibility. Also,

> *Used well, strategy meetings provide clarity and momentum. They align a team around key decisions and create positive energy. Used poorly, strategy meetings irritate people. They waste time and energy, or worse, strengthens entrenched points of view creating frustration and resignation.*[2]

---

[2] Sundheim, Doug. "3 Reasons Your Strategy Meetings Irritate Your Team." *Harvard Business Review*. March 01, 2016. Accessed November 19, 2018. https://hbr.org/2016/03/3-reasons-your-strategy-meetings-irritate-your-team

When strategic planning is not undertaken with inclusivity, everyone in the organization is left feeling frustrated by the process after so much time and so many resources, including an emotional toll, have been invested. Often, you hear people say afterward, "No matter what, it never seems to gain any momentum."

Employees may be lost during the implementation phase if they do not know how to participate effectively. Those who are inclusive and do it differently, as we will see, have a much greater opportunity to become examples of success stories when it comes to implementation of the strategy.

It is not a coincidence I aspired to write a book about strategy. I wanted to share what I have learned and my passion for researching, scrutinizing, and appreciating strategy and strategic implementation. I have been curious about and interested in how we can improve the workings of any organization for three decades.

I personally have experienced the agony and defeat, and the joy and exhilaration, of being on three sides of the strategic game; the development of a new strategy, strategic implementation, and consulting. I have been the receiver of the strategic directive and the creator of the strategic directive.

I am an advocate of driving our local and global economy by ensuring nano cap[3] and privately held organizations (companies below $50 million) build effective strategies, strategic implementation plans, and operational efficiencies.

During my tenure with one of the largest health care organizations, I had the responsibility of opening three new, major hospitals and consulted with another major hospital in Los Angeles. After working on the three hospitals, and prior to consulting on the fourth, I spent time as the assistant hospital administrator (vice president of operations). I held full oversight responsibilities over strategic business management activities for security, engineering, facilities, clinical technology, food and nutrition, supply chain management, environmental services, and health and safety. And I strategically and tactically collaborated with all other hospital departments, regional and national leadership, and external vendors.

Leading large-scale projects and then operations, it became very apparent that meeting time and budget requirements requires a clear and concise strategy, a very

---

[3] "A nano cap refers to small, publicly traded companies with a market capitalization below $50 million. Nano cap is as small as you can get in terms of market capitalization. Nano cap present a high degree of investment risk. This is important to understand as they have a limited history in the market, and as a result, it is difficult to track performance. The best way to understand the quality and performance of nano cap is to look at the fundamentals of the company, the underlying business operations and sector, and specific assets, performance, and plans for the future." (www.investinganswers.com) Chen, James. "Nano Cap" Investopediacom. January 21, 2017 Accessed November 19, 2019. https://www.investopedia.com/terms/n/nanocap.asp

specific implementation plan, and a great deal of planning and managing to the outcomes. As another note, focusing on doing the real work, prioritizing the work, and finding new ways to do the work are all imperative.

The pursuit of the success of these projects was a reflection of the entire team who led the way. The core team incisively planned, stayed calm, kept cool, managed deadlines, stayed flexible, and drove for outcomes aligned with overarching strategy. The other 200 teams required clear plans, specific goals, and outcomes driven by specific dates. These teams required a great deal of facilitation, follow up, and communication.

Executive leadership experience is second only to my consulting work.

During this time, I used many new concepts, leveraging innovative ways to move the strategy forward, and I want to share a few of them with you. I will highlight them here, but they will be explained further throughout the book.

One of the ideas which worked well and I have used again and again: Share the overall strategy and gather *all* of the right people in the room to build department operational plans. Then be sure to share the plan with all of the other teams, and based on cross-learning, make changes to the individual department implementation plans. Bring people together, have everyone roll up their sleeves, and make a day of it. Do not shortchange this activity. When you are counting on a collection of information and plans, the more you cross-share, the better the outcomes and the faster the implementation.

Another idea: Leverage what I now call Operational Action Response Teams (OARTs). This is a modified concept of how action response teams operate. The OART is a new kind of team with a mix of members to assist in driving momentum in real time that produces an employee experience, helps make quick microshifts, and reduces barriers to leadership's access and information.

As a strategic leader, it was important in my work that I balanced equal parts friendly and fierce, cerebral and ruthless, master and apprentice, and be unstoppable—then any strategic game could be won.

Then, when it was all said and done—with successes and failures under my belt—I knew it was time, and I desired a new path. So after more than a decade at the health care company, I set off on a new journey. My goal: to share my knowledge of people, process, and profits through improving strategy and strategic implementation by being an advisor to C-suite executives, entrepreneurs, and founders.

Now, let's move into how to fix the eight great ways strategies fail.

PART II

How To Fix The Eight Great Ways Strategies Fail

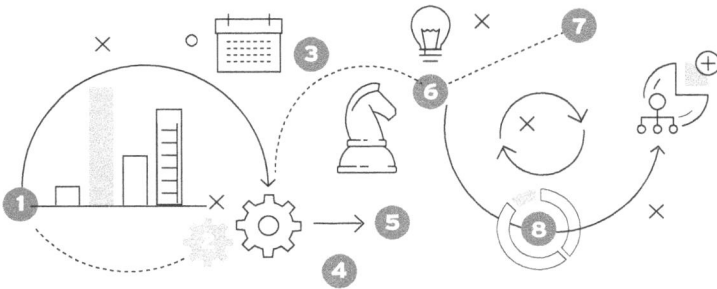

CHAPTER 3

· ·

Failure #1:
Not Connecting
Mission To Strategy

A major misstep is when the strategy is created with no direct connection to the organization's mission, vision, values, or culture. Strategy is intended to drive toward desired business results, and if your end results are not interconnected to your mission, vision, values, and culture, implementation will not happen.

In simplistic form: the mission, vision, and values answer the question, "Why does the business exist and how do we make decisions?" These need to be clearly written, defined, and understood by everyone involved in the organization, including vendors and customers. There should be no wavering.

Culture is the spirit of the organization. Unless one of the strategic initiatives is to change the overall organizational culture, you need to align the how-to with the current culture.

We all know instinctively whether there is a strong or weak culture within an organization, but no matter what, culture beats strategy every single time. You should never underestimate the time needed to discuss cultural implications during strategic planning sessions. The success rate of execution will go up exponentially if you have examined and noted the pros and cons of the culture in relation to each and every strategic initiative and implementation method. Specifically, highlight cultural information in your communication plan, because you cannot assume people will make the desired connections.

In today's environment, the most effective executive knows to embrace the idea that a great strategy is not just the product of the hours spent producing a plan unrelated to the existing state of the organization. Instead, it is the result of a rough-and-ready process of thinking through what it would take to achieve the desired priorities, and then taking the time to assess whether it is a realistic and workable plan that will drive toward the mission, vision, and values. Effective executives will further inquire, "Can the plan be implemented within the confines of the organizational culture," and "Who else needs to be involved in the discussion to provide the practicalities of implementing the desired strategic agenda?"

Changing The Way We Think About Strategy

I think as part of ensuring this coordinated connection between strategy and mission, vision, values, and culture, we must change our language. In part, *language* is keeping us from making the necessary connections. In a way, we should get away from adding the word *plan* to strategic plan because it implies stasis. The truth is that no strategy is static.

Instead of strategy being a *thing* (or *another thing*) that we feel we have to do, we should shift our thinking from building it as an inert and stagnant plan into a potent and lively document that reflects the fluidity of the culture. Let us think about changing the word *planning* contained in the phrase "strategic planning" to words like *intention, system, procedure, undertaking,* and *commitment*—much more encompassing.

What if we stopped putting the strategy in a spiral-bound book, making charts, and sending it out via emails? What if we went out and talked to the very people who were expected to execute the strategy? Why not build a culture of people who want to pledge or promise to do whatever it takes (within the law and reason) to get it done?

CEOs and entrepreneurs need to vow to make strategy a living, breathing piece of work that lives up to the mission, vision, and values—a place where art and science converge. A family owned-business needs to do the same.

- What if we used the term *strategic intention* to mean the determination to act? Now it becomes strategic acting. Now it becomes an opportunity for people to execute on the plan at the heart of the culture.

- What if we used the term *strategic system* to mean a set of connected parts forming a complex whole, a collection of pieces working together to create momentum? Now it becomes inclusive of the entire corporate ecosystem with no area (unless the exclusion is intentional) left untouched or unrecognized.

- What if we used the term *strategic procedure* to mean establishing an official way of doing things, thus creating a series of systems and processes conducted in a particular order or manner? Now we have movement toward getting the real work done. No guessing, no inaction, no frustration. *Bam*! Now we are living the vision.

- What if we used the term *strategic undertaking* to mean a formal pledge, promise, and/or oath to do a task? Everyone would take a vow toward the implementation efforts. *Awesome*! Now we are living the mission.

- What if we used the term *strategic commitment* to mean the state of being dedicated to a cause, an allegiance? Now we will have created a workforce that is present. Everyone shows up as expected because they know the community of committed individuals will be let down if they do not. *Awe-inspiring*! Now we are living the values.

ACTIONABLE SHIFTS

1. Strategic Implementation requires Operational Action Response Teams (described later), dynamic staff meetings that are run differently and supplemented by quick huddles.

2. Focus on and define only what is important to the organization and forget the rest.

3. Always keep the implementation at the forefront of the conversation.

4. Eliminate resistance and barriers by constantly paying attention to input from others.

5. Simplify the strategy so it is focused and directed toward outcomes that are aligned with the culture.

6. Regularly review data within the confines of the strategic drivers. Make sure to measure and examine outcomes continuously, not only

when preparing for the strategic planning session.

7. When in development, be inclusive: create teams from a mixed group of people to come up with new ideas and then vet the feasibility of those ideas according to the reality of implementation success factors.

8. Clarify the meanings and actions for those who wish to live the vision, mission, and values, so employees understand what behaviors they are to exhibit. That level of clarification will help when they are working on and implementing the strategy.

9. Explicitly call out the organizational culture. Overestimate the need to explain the expected behaviors and call out the hidden cultural norms and rituals, so employees do not undermine the work during implementation.

10. Be sure to define the parameters regarding how creative or noncreative you expect people to be—from your C-suite to the front line.

If executives adopt these definitions, then maybe, just maybe, they can keep strategy where it should be: simple, plausible, and implementable.

CHAPTER 4

•••

Failure #2:
Pushing Strategies
Down From The Top

T his trap is perhaps the most insidious because it can snare even the smartest and most experienced executives trying to build an implementable strategy. In identifying and articulating a strategy, executives adopt the typical standard framework, doing it themselves with their closest confidants.

When this happens, work is done without having all of the right players at the table. This isolation is quite disheartening to loyal employees since they also want to drive toward accomplishing the mission. But if there is organizational detachment from those loyal employees, they cannot engage in the needed forward movement toward any of the organizational goals, momentum is never achieved, and they are likely to become disengaged from the process altogether. As a result, you will soon notice a high level of absenteeism or presenteeism—a warm body in a seat, but no one is home or participating in the process.

Absenteeism is estimated to cost in the range of $80 billion[4] annually in lost productivity. Presenteeism losses are estimated to be ten times higher than absenteeism, estimated at around $150 billion[5]. It was disheartening to listen to one founder of a $6 million company explain to me that he feared he would never be able to grow the company, and maybe it would even decline, because his employees thought nothing of calling off work at the last moment. He did not want to be thought of as a "mean" boss, so he allowed for a culture of absenteeism—some say this culture also creates a culture of presenteeism. But what I saw for sure was he was losing all of his outstanding employees, who were caught in the trap of continuously covering for others.

Together, we created a communications plan sharing with people the amount of money it was costing the organization, what is meant for them as employees, built in new accountabilities, and implemented daily huddles. It took over a year, but he began to see the shift. In addition, those who could not live up to the expectations were asked to find work someplace else.

---

[4] Folger, Jean. "Causes and Costs of Absenteeism". Investopedia.com. April 16, 2018. Accessed November 19, 2019.

[5] Smith, Sandi. "Phoning It In: Do You Know How Much Presenteeism Costs Your Business?" Ehstoday.com. January 21, 2016. Accessed November 19, 2019.

I believe the reluctance to bring an array of people to the strategic table is based on fear of divulging too much information or letting people know the *dirty laundry* and weak points. Another reason is the need or desire of executives to adopt only ideas and concepts that can be carefully controlled. During isolated strategy discussions, for example, energy is often focused on specific customers to target and how to create a value proposition for those customers, instead of inviting others to broaden the ideas for future growth.

In some businesses, there is also a negative attitude to overcome regarding employees. Upper management may believe that lower-tier staff members do not understand the processes of doing business or the constraints that may be in effect. This same belief prompts the idea that employees may end up with unrealistic expectations, and it often prevents upper management from allowing employees to know the ins and outs of operations.

I also think for some businesses, it sometimes feels as if a thorough explanation will take too much time and effort and is a longer process than leaders are willing to engage in.

It Is All About Your People

I suggest that you involve the people if you want effective engagement and smooth implementation of strategy. Yes, it certainly takes some extra time, but that up-front investment means less time and money will be spent on the back end due to slow execution—and slow is detrimental, especially when you want to leverage your competitive advantage. People want to be heard; then they want to be understood; then they want a follow-up; then they want to know why you agreed or disagreed with their ideas. In the end, employees want to be a part of the greater overall success. So, bring others into the process, and they will take ownership of their performance for the company.

These actions are not a one-time proposition, either—they will be an ongoing part of the process.

What if you made strategy an ongoing conversation in the sense of articulating, implementing, checking in, rearticulating, implementing, checking in…? When you have involved others up front and avoided the direct, top-down approach, people will self-correct much faster, and then, when something is not going according to plan, you will also know it faster. Sometimes, as a leader, you just need to engage differently. I did the moonwalk down the hallway, music blasting and staff lined up. I had promised the department I would if they could find a few cost savings strategies—and they came up with several outstanding ones. Silly may not always be the answer, but we can't keep doing the same thing.

No more asking yourself, "How did we get so far down the path before we knew it was not working?" No more listening to someone say, "We have already spent millions of dollars, so we are not going to change the direction." This type of thinking causes company projects to continue to fail. Celebrate the success and do things differently moving forward.

ACTIONABLE INVOLVEMENT

1. Strategic Implementation requires Operational Action Response Teams (described later), dynamic staff meetings that are run differently and supplemented by quick huddles.

2. Focus on and define only what is important to the organization and forget the rest.

3. Always keep the implementation at the forefront of the conversation.

4. Eliminate resistance and barriers by constantly paying attention to input from others.

5. Simplify the strategy so it is focused and directed toward outcomes that are aligned with the culture.

6. Regularly review data within the confines of the strategic drivers. Make sure to measure and examine outcomes continuously, not only when preparing for the strategic planning session.

7. When in development, be inclusive: create teams from a mixed group of people to come up with new ideas and then vet the feasibility of those ideas according to the reality of implementation success factors.

8. Clarify the meanings and actions for those who wish to live the vision, mission, and values, so employees understand what behaviors they are to exhibit. That level of clarification will help when they are working on and implementing the strategy.

9. Explicitly call out the organizational culture. Overestimate the need to explain the expected behaviors and call out the hidden cultural norms and rituals, so employees do not undermine the work during implementation.

10. Be sure to define the parameters regarding how creative or noncreative you expect people to be—from your C-suite to the front line.

If executives adopt these definitions, then maybe, just maybe, they can keep strategy where it should be: simple, plausible, and implementable.

CHAPTER 5

•••

Failure #3: Not Understanding The Real Meaning Of Strategy

Unfortunately, the strategy concept has been diluted to the point that people toss it out there and brand themselves as strategic thinkers.

It is easy to fall into the trap. "I get it, so others should get it." Boards, C-suite executives, and entrepreneurs spend the majority of their time hearing the term *strategy* and then thinking about their own interpretation of the idea.

Strategy is now such a commonly heard word that the assumption is everyone understands it. Some people seem highly comfortable with its planning and discussion aspects and spend lots of time reviewing and approving ideas—others, not so much.

Management and board discussions focused on how to squeeze more revenue out of existing profit centers and how to generate new revenue sources are now commonplace. The metrics of finance, production, and capabilities are common concerns and discussion points. The upper levels of leadership are constantly in the thick of it while those who are required to make it happen, to do the real work, are assigned, by default, the back seat in their levels of understanding. Afterward, they are also typically criticized when implementation fails. Everyone has heard of the law of physics; everything rolls downhill and gains momentum—even on gravity hills.[6]

Because this problem is primarily rooted in people's naturalaversiontotakingthingsdeliberatelyandrespectfully overcommunicating, things become less cohesive and misunderstood farther down the organizational chart. The ideal approach to implementation involves taking the essential time needed to over-explain, including defining what the strategy is, what it means, and what success will look like to all members of the group.

Failure to take the time to take those steps means the project could potentially fail. Strategy implementation (because we throw those words around) often results in employees simply hearing *empty* words. If people do not know what the words translate into and are intended to create, or if they relate to the words they hear from a shallow level of motivation, such as *what is in it for me* (WIIFM), they may not ever arrive at an executable perspective on how to do the tactical work, so they are unsuccessful.

---

[6] "Gravity Hill." Wikipedia. October 16, 2018. Accessed November 19, 2018. https://en.wikipedia.org/wiki/Gravity_hill.

I will take an even bolder step—the majority of people who are throwing the words around are *themselves* unlikely to know the true meaning of strategic concepts as they relate to their organizations.

Escaping The Misunderstanding

The only remedy for an incomplete organizational understanding of strategy is to adopt a discipline of strategy, accepting that there is and always will be misunderstandings, and that everyone will experience some levels of angst. The solution involves ensuring that everyone stops throwing around terms that are meaningless unless specificity encompasses those terms.

At all levels of the organization, leadership should challenge, explain, and reiterate guidance when it comes to concern about conformity to rules, concerns about what others do and "how it is done." Egos must, by necessity, be removed. There should be no attitude of "We get it, so why don't they?" or "Why should we need to define it?" and definitely no more "They are the issue, not me." The days of "I got this" must be over.

Maintaining this shift in ideals and ideas may not be easy since staying in one's own comfort zone is always easier and more comfortable. It will be important, however, to remember that these principles are the keys to creating and implementing a successful strategy.

Understanding and defining the organizational life cycle can assist leaders in explaining the state of the organization, why decisions are made, what some of the driving forces behind the decision-making process are, and how to accept—not absorb—the sensations of frenzy, frustration, or failure that may arise.

Understanding and defining the types of strategy is the first step of understanding the quagmire of terms. There are so many strategies, and organizational leaders need to decipher these terms within their own context to get clear on what they mean for their particular organization, and address the process with clarity.

ACTIONABLE CLARITY

1. Those who are identified as strategic need to make sure that those doing the work are correctly aligned and doing the right tactical work.

2. An organization needs to be very clear on how, when, and why it uses the term strategy and implementation (or execution).

3. Define the terms strategy and implementation as they are expected to be interpreted within your organization.

4. Stop identifying yourself or others as a strategic thinker and instead reinterpret the role as someone who is a definer of strategy or an implementer of strategy.

5. Get out of the head-and-heart state of mind, roll up your sleeves, and be laser-focused on what is important: actions, reactions, and the process of just getting it done.

6. Study the state of the organization and create implementable plans that work within the stages of the organizational life cycle.

7. Become comfortable with uncertainty and know ahead of time that a certain amount of anxiety is part of the process, no matter how well-defined the plan may be.

8. Embrace misunderstandings, since they can eventually lead to more clarity.

9. Slow down to speed up when it comes to explaining and communicating both terms and the expected outcomes.

10. Explicitly explain the concept of WIIFM.

CHAPTER 6

•••

Failure #4:
Neglecting The
Critical Few

There is a far too common and false belief everyone in the organization should be classed as strategic. If this is the case, then everyone in the organization feels the need to *be* strategic, holding on to power and control. But if *everyone* thinks they are strategic and there continues to be a strong misunderstanding of what strategic means, there is no wonder that failure of implementation is so high; *someone* needs to do the tactical work.

Executives sometimes give the false sense to their entire employee population that they are all allowed to be strategic, instead of being courageous enough to say, "You will be the people to get the work done." They neglect to be clear regarding who the strategic drivers are and who the implementers are. In good practice, leaders should be clear on how the employees play a key role in *working the plan* to accomplish the desired objectives.

Staff members believe if they are strategic or think strategically, they will have an increased level of influence over their world. *Nope.* They do not.

Strategic or not, everyone has a certain level of influence within his or her particular environment—that influence can be used for positive or negative. Being strategic has nothing to do with one's influence. I do believe influence is critical to any work environment. Executives must find, encourage, and leverage the people who are positive influencers. But listening to the negative influencers is also important because you can learn a lot from them. Just do not let them become the ones who are driving the plans forward. In fact, you may discover you end up needing their assistance to garner commitment. If it is not working out with them, however, and they cannot be persuaded to do good by getting on board, then moving them entirely out of the organization quickly is a far better plan than worrying about what their level of influence on others might be.

Without clarity regarding who is to be strategic, the power of execution can be misplaced due to direct action driven by executives, by circumstance, through a crisis, or by default. If there is one place not to give up your power and influence, it is here.

Eliminate The Rogue

Leaders must have followers and implementers. Be clear and concise with every level of the organization including executives, employees, subcontractors, vendors, and clients about where the strategy is held and who is responsible for implementation. This direction must also include the *what*—behaviors and outcomes that are expected of each person.

Some people are necessarily tactical, and an explanation must be clearly given to them regarding how each person's tactical work drives the strategy. Tactics move the strategy forward, and those who are in tactical roles are critical to the organization. The days of the ivory tower are over; it is essential to meet with employees to reassure them when they are doing the right thing and quickly course-correct when they are not.

Personal campaigns can derail the process and ultimately destroy a company. A well-meaning employee (or saboteur) with a loud voice and an extensive internal social network can drive the organization in the wrong direction. That type of behavior must be stopped before it accelerates by discontinuing any impromptu meetings that arise after official strategy planning meetings—periods when people do Monday morning quarterbacking undermine the decisions of the board of directors, C-Suite and entrepreneurs.

Egotistical departmental bosses also sometimes attempt to override the CEO's direction, and as a result, they may destroy previous work done to create the plan. These are often likable and charming people; they may have what appears to be good relationships with the people beneath and parallel to them and an extensive knowledge of company practices. Look more deeply, however, and you will notice they frequently wear a mask of passive-aggression and they cannot manage to put their carefully chosen words into concrete action. Their sole aim may be to hold onto what power they currently have and undermine anyone else's input.

I once observed an unfortunate situation in which an experienced, seasoned CEO was hoodwinked by the type of person described above—I will call him John. John was a senior vice president who led three departments and about 100 people. John was well-read and could quote extensively from any leadership book. He would come to executive leadership meetings, regurgitate statistics, and liked to tell others how they should solve their problems because he had already experienced the same situation. He spent a lot of time in the CEO's office schmoozing and telling little white lies. When asked a direct question by anyone, he would make a bold and confident statement, but never actually answered the question that was asked. The CEO spent many meetings praising how well John was doing with all of his departments. Then, John was promoted and another person took over his departments. When the new leader took over, he found that all three departments were significantly out of compliance, were not coordinating the strategies set forth, and would finish the year way over budget. When it was further investigated by the Human Resource Department, the theme emerged: John was egotistical and was holding power over people by being a bully. Many people were afraid of him. Thus causing them to be paralyzed producing a culture of inaction and miss-direction.

Now that HR became heavily involved with John's behavior, the CEO was forced to take action. When I spoke to the CEO, he shared with me, "When I really think about it, I knew there was something wrong." He continued, "Basically I ignored my intuition, that gut feeling I had, and the information I had received I just brushed it off." He had received many negative reports from others about John he ignored. The issue, he *liked* John—lesson learned: likability does not always equal good leadership. But because it was easier to just keep the status quo, the CEO never thought it was going to turn as bad as it did.

Switching gears. Do you have influencers in your organization? There are people with executive titles who can be influencers. However, I believe the best and most powerful influencers are those who do not sit in the executive offices. They are the employees who work throughout the ranks of the organization. By identifying the influencers and then nurturing their abilities they can exponentially help move the organization forward in the correct strategic direction.

Carly was one of those influencers who worked in a department I led. Through conversations, I found out she was well-liked by her peers. She was well respected because she was knowledgeable about the tasks at hand, she took the time to help her colleagues, she was cheerful, and she never spoke a bad word about any of her co-workers or leaders.

When I, out of necessity, had to make a significant change to the staff's schedules, I solicited input from Carly. She asked thoughtful and respectful questions, as she wanted to be very clear about the objectives and impacts it would make on the department and staff. She and I knew there was going to be a lot of unhappy employees since it meant they would either need to come in earlier or stay later. After Carly clearly understood the reasons for the change, she helped me articulate and explain the reasoning to the staff. She became an unofficial sponsor of the change. Her influence was extremely effective in making this transition easier and in a shorter time frame. A side note, in addition to Carly helping the organization through this change and by me paying attention to who had influence and how they would handle themselves helped me decide who would be the next supervisor for the department—of course, Carly.

ACTIONABLE FOCUS

1. Explain the division of labor and role assignments to those who are chosen—who will be in charge of driving the strategy, who will be driving implementation, and who will be accountable for tactics.

2. Discuss this plan with each executive individually and outline your expectations for the execution of the plan.

3. Set guidelines for your executives to assist them as they find key people who will report to them and have the same conversation about executing the strategy and being tactical.

4. Be very clear and specific about your process for selection and who is selected, since not everyone will be chosen to drive the strategy.

5. Identify those you believe should be doing the tactical work. These are the people who are getting the real work done.

6. Job task clarity is critical.

7. Follow up with everyone to ensure each person is behaving appropriately and "staying in their lane."

8. Do not allow egotistical employees or power-hungry types to creep in and change the direction.

9. For the utmost in clarity, follow up as often as necessary, so the work you are expecting is being done correctly. Create ongoing opportunities for clarity throughout the ecosystem of the organization

10. Never underestimate the power of an internal influencer within the organization, either for good or evil.

CHAPTER 7

•••

Failure #5:
Failure To Maintain
Focused Momentum

S trategy is a loaded word; in some areas, it is like a lead balloon hitting the floor. Too often, people overhear discussion of "the strategy," but lack of prior information or warning that changes are afoot may create confusion within the organization and result in a lack of energy surrounding the execution. Additionally, employees may then sit through a presentation about the organization's strategy and take the easiest route afterward, staying in their personal comfort zones, doing only what they have always done.

If the strategy implementation plan is not communicated well, the majority of information stops at the mid-level leaders in the organization, and even they are not always clear about actionable steps that are needed, or how to communicate the plan to their staff. If there *is* communication, it is kept at such high levels that no one knows exactly what roles they play or what the success factors are considered to be in relation to their job.

Without measurable performance indicators throughout the entire organization, although the plan has been created, it is too often expected to be magically implemented. The strategic plan may stop at a list of objectives and general tactics if key performance indicators (KPIs) are not developed.

Perhaps the strategy is perceived as a *flavor-of-the-month* proposition. The faster the world moves, the more we desire to change our strategy. But it may not be our *strategy* that should be rapidly changing—it should be our *tactics.* Often, if the execution tactics were not correctly aligned with the strategy, the strategy itself is blamed for not working. If there was a failure to communicate effectively, the wrong work might have been done, and then the employees are blamed.

A thicker-than-necessary strategic plan and implementation plan has, in the past, become a badge of honor—the more words and ideas that come out of the planning sessions, the better. Worse yet is the concept of keeping the plan in your head if you are at upper levels of management and not communicating down through the ranks. Entrepreneurs and leaders of family-run business are more frequently guilty of not having any plan at all.

No matter the type or size of the company, the preferred method for such plans should be KISS (Keep It Simple and Succinct).

A Force To Be Reckoned With

A company's strategic choices cannot be summarized in one or two pages using simple words and concepts for a few reasons. Characterizing the key choices as simply as possible—where to play and how to win—keeps the discussion grounded and makes it more likely that managers will engage with the strategic challenges the firm faces instead of retreating to their planning comfort zone.

Communication (yes, another severely over-used word) bears mentioning, especially in relation to the concept of talking *at* someone versus genuine dialogue that involves discussing ideas and concepts. Instead of dictating the strategy down to people and then hoping the tactical work gets done correctly, leaders need to have precise execution discussions with their people. For every department and at every staffing level, there needs to be a well-defined communication plan for strategy implementation.

If it is left up to the people in the organization to guess which metrics are important and which ones will drive the organization forward, you may get some sort of result, but it is unlikely to be what you wanted. Every individual should have a measurable indicator of success that is directly related to individual tactical outcomes. This approach drives the departmental strategy and also drives the company strategy in the correct direction.

It is time-consuming to create key performance indicators (KPIs) that cascade throughout the organization, but I believe people prefer to perform to a standard of measure, and they want to do the right work for the right reason. In fact, if they are doing the wrong work, and they discover that fact, a serious state of demotivation will ensue.

Did I remember to mention that everyone needs KPIs?

The influence factor cannot be overstated. Here is an influence equation: Influence is a factor of experience times relationships squared plus power:

$$I = f(E \times R^2)P$$

Either you get the experience, or you surround yourself with people who have the experience and then build the relationships.

As a part of the influence equation, I would also say power plays a significant part in the success factor. We should never underestimate the power that is derived simply due to a title. But people will see right through that if the person with power approaches the leadership role through their title alone, not through charisma or ability to interact effectively with others. Know your formal and informal power quotient.

All leaders today are feeling the escalating necessity of robust "employee experience" strategies (oh no—*another strategy*). Creating these experiences requires a new and different blend of face-to-face dialogue, technology interaction, and meetings.

I have been successful at moving multimillion-dollar projects forward using a modified concept of how action response teams operate. I have used this approach successfully within health care, IT, construction, and other industries. The implementation of Operational Action Response Teams (OARTs) serves to (1) create the employee experience, (2) help the organization make quick microshifts that assist with the execution of key performance indicators, and (3) reduce the barriers to leadership access and information.

The OART is a new kind of team with a mix of members to assist in driving momentum. OARTs move throughout the organization to answer questions, solve problems, and identify resources that are needed. The use of OARTs eliminates the delayed process of not getting things done, bringing visibility and actionable response, so the tactics required to implement the strategy can constantly be at the forefront of everyone's mind. OARTs are not about seeking what is wrong, but looking for what is right, empowering the team, determining how to make microshifts promptly, and listening to what is getting in the way of execution.

The team needs to be well-versed in the organization's systems, processes, policies, culture, values, etc. Team members may need to simply clarify a policy involving the function or flow of a process. They may need to simply motivate and inspire, or congratulate a department. They should let employees boast about their area and discuss their concerns. This type of process serves to build a culture of engagement and trust, instead of allowing it to deteriorate into a "complaint hearing" that lacks a positive outcome.

The team needs to be politically savvy and able to guide people in a positive way, but also able to listen and take action on barriers to execution. Sometimes, the team moves in as a collective mentor or guide. This is different than the senior team that does rounds or the regulatory team that inspects for safety issues; this is a team of people who help solve issues in real time. When they do not know the answer, then within twenty-four hours, they must return with concrete information.

As an example, if an OART puts a solution team together, it should then expect to have the issue fully resolved within a week. It is important to be on top of the situation and stick to commitments. Fail once, and it may take forever to recover.

These solution teams should never be operating at the same time, on the same day, or on the same shift. If you have a twenty-four-hour operation, then say hello to 2:00 a.m.

To encourage the success of the OART, the process should include a method of tracking and reporting the outcomes of team activities directly to the CEO. I suggest you choose a person who is well respected in the organization (not necessarily the person whose title seems to indicate they should lead it). Be careful not to select the "teacher's pet" staff member and spend time carefully choosing the team members; make sure, as well, you have chosen people who can live up to and meet the influence equation.

ACTIONABLE MOVEMENT

1. Communication is the number one way to drive the right work at the right time and also sustain the necessary level of momentum.

2. Those leading your communication department need to be involved from the earliest stages of the planning. They are not an afterthought.

3. It is up to the leader to create opportunities for a dynamic conversation with the team regarding the plan and what it means for everyone. This includes explaining each person's role in the strategy's success and tactical implementation.

4. Check and verify the strategy. Is it driving to meet your core competitive advantage? If yes, then check how the workforce is driving to meet the strategy. Maybe the employees are working hard, but in the wrong direction.

5. Implement the Operational Action Response Team concept into the organization.

6. Take time to celebrate each true success, because those successes that can be seen as real progress. Celebrate individuals, teams, and departments. A word to the wise though— do not celebrate activities that are merely normal daily operations; staff will soon come to expect it. Be sure celebrations are for true opportunities worth celebrating.

7. Learn to listen to both what is being said and what is not being said. In other words, read between the lines.

8. Pay special attention to what the naysayers are saying and take note of how they are behaving. Help them change their behavior and bring them on board—or get them out altogether. Please note that this is not a recommendation to give them attention, but to pay attention. Spend time with the true champions and pay special attention to the top 10 percent of your performers.

9. Acknowledge there are ebbs and flows to momentum. No organization can keep the engine revved up all of the time. Give it a break and then rev it up again. In other words, take a deep breath every once in a while.

10. Remember, often a simple conversation with your team allows you to engage or re-engage enthusiasm. Leverage your experience, relationships, and power to influence your employees to keep up the great work and momentum.

CHAPTER 8

••

Failure #6: Squander The Resources

Strategy execution requires a variety of resources. Sometimes, executives are busy creating a grand strategy that will provide the company with boundless strides forward, but it is done without considering the available resources. Thus, metaphorically, it is like trying to hammer a square peg into a round hole—it just will not work without some destruction.

Everyone knows resources are not always about the green stuff—an infusion of money is not always the solution. Attempting to accomplish your strategy may be hindered by something altogether different—maybe it is suboptimal flow and function of departments and operations, and funding will be required to make required changes. Not having the right mix of equipment or talent can also generate significant expense.

Obtaining and appropriately allocating required resources plays a key role in the success or failure of strategy. By providing the required resources, you are essentially building a level of trust so that everyone can successfully participate in the execution of the strategy.

But building trust is a two-way street. Providing resources for employees to get the work done is critical, and in turn, the employees acting fiscally responsible by getting the work completed is an equally important part of the success of the organization.

Not providing enough resources is a sure-fire way of crushing any trust that currently exists in an organization. If you do not give employees resources, money, time, equipment, systems, processes, and other necessary success factors, then implementation is unquestionably going to fail. Expect comments like, "Once again, they expect us to get it done with what?" (or worse yet, "Forget it; I am tired of being the one that has to suffer"). And then there is this one: "They are squeezing it all out of me, so I am just going to work slower and not harder." This takes us right back to the issues of absenteeism or presenteeism.

Leaders often underestimate the time and money it will take to implement. It is better to go after fewer objectives and get them right than more and only achieve mediocrity. In such cases, more will never be interpreted as better. To ensure resources are being allocated correctly, conduct implementation meetings identifying the key performance indicators and ensuring enough resources have been allocated.

I have observed companies go out of business because the CEO's ego got in the way and he (or she) would not prioritize or let go of a pet project. In such cases, the project uses up resources that could be better spent on critical priorities.

Another costly area is talent. It is difficult to let the *one you like* go. But it is important to hire slow and fire fast.

Do not count on resources you do not have yet. If you do not have the million-dollar project in the bank, then do not plan as if you do. I have been in the room when an executive said, "Don't worry. We are going to close the deal in thirty days, so let's just go ahead and purchase the capital equipment for expansion." And then, as the equipment arrived, the other company decided to not move forward with the anticipated contract. I had tried to forewarn them—but what came next? Layoffs. The organization needed to cover the cost of the equipment.

This is not meant to discourage you from making projections and plans for when you *do* get the contract, but do not move ahead recklessly, bet the farm, and risk the survivability of the organization on something that has not yet been acquired.

Remember, do not take on too many objectives and goals. Pay attention to progress and how resources are being consumed. When you see something is not working, be willing and ready to pull the plug before hundreds of thousands of dollars are wasted and the entire workforce is demotivated. Let it go and accept the sunk costs.

Show Me The Resource

One significant resource that needs to be accounted for is giving people *time* to understand the direction or new direction of the organization. What this looks like is up for discussion and is based on the size and complexity of the organization or project. Failure to provide the time to absorb and process the information may result in employees who become disconnected and uncommitted. Of course, these types of initiatives will require capital support.

Money. Yes, the actual green stuff.

- Bring in the right person or persons to make this analysis.

- Create complete what-if scenarios.

- Plan for the best and worst-case situations.

- Be sure to include contingency funds.

- Share the budget with people and let them know the full extent of the risks and rewards.

By the way, when you share the budget, speak in terms that allow people to understand how they can impact the financial health of the organization. As executives, we are accustomed to talking in terms of large numbers, frequently in the millions. But remember, a front-line staff member might barely be able to put food on the table. Some have to choose between feeding their children and putting roofs over their heads. Front-line staff will not be able to fully comprehend when you say, "We only have a million dollars to accomplish this project." They may say, albeit in their heads, "Do you know what I could do with a million dollars?" Be aware that it is important to be sensitive to their individual situations. I found out once that one of my employees was living in a car because he was getting a divorce, could only afford a place for his soon to be ex-wife and kids, could not afford a second place to live with the children, and did not want the kids to be out on the street.

Talk to your staff with respect and in terms they can understand. For example, I had to explain to front-line workers that I needed to cut the budget by a million dollars. So I held up three one-dollar bills and said, "I currently have three dollars to run this department, but I need to reduce it by one dollar to two dollars." I continued: "…and I need your help. You are the experts in this department. Can you help me find savings?"

Guess what? They instantly did. They helped reduce the budget, we created additional efficiencies, the staff became more engaged, and yes, we celebrated because they went above and beyond their regular duties. As a side note, a few of the staff came up to me later and said, "We have never been asked to tell anyone what was wrong. Thank you."

An analysis of *systems and processes* should be ongoing all of the time. An assessment and reassessment should be woven into the fabric of the organization. The Operational Action Response Team can be a great influence in this area. Go to the staff, consult with them, and they will tell it like it is and will help make it happen if you give them a chance.

Having the *right workforce and the right people* is critical. A total revamp of your organizational chart might be in order. Yes, this might also mean you need to change the makeup of your workforce, moving people out of their current roles and into others or possibly letting go of people. Human Resources needs to be an early adopter of this strategy, so hiring practices can be aligned and able to accommodate a change in candidate recruiting. Departments must be part of the overall effort to hire a workforce that is aligned with the strategy from the very beginning. This may mean reorganizing the HR department for the total health of the organization.

ACTIONABLE KA-CHING

1. Take the time to understand the reality of what it will take to make things happen—validate timing and financial constraints.

2. Do not force change or processes into an existing system and workflow.

3. Keep the people involved to balance the real truth of operational functions and flows.

4. Create systems to validate the reality of the proposed idea fitting into the organization.

5. Create feedback loops so when there is an issue, quick changes can be made and course corrections are more effective.

6. Create opportunities through huddles, roundtables, and check-ins to ensure that implementation is not derailed.

7. Be a more intuitive leader by listening to rumors and water-cooler conversations. Take note of the information, do not react hastily, and incorporate it into the plan to overcome any issues so others can effectively carry out the directives. This approach will help you overcome barriers and risks to implementation. Do not avoid negative chatter—learn from it.

8. Be a champion of listening. The more you listen, the more you know—and the more you gather additional champions and influencers, the faster the implementation happens.

9. Bring finance people into the conversation early and often. Know the numbers.

10. Be willing to pull the plug on an idea because you do not have the right resources or the timing is not right. Resist the temptation to try and push forward to make it happen with what you have, and within the current circumstances you are facing.

CHAPTER 9

•••

Failure #7:
Misalign Function
And Flow

During the strategic planning session, great ideas are generated, and people frequently think they have produced the ultimate strategic plan. However, the plan is often intended to move forward in a totally opposite direction from the reality of the situation. What initially excited everyone falls flat, and then people begin to talk about what a waste of time and money it was to spend three days sequestered together.

There are often situations in which input from others has been specifically solicited, and then nothing is communicated back after an assessment. Or the input is completely ignored, the opposite reaction is achieved, and anger ensues—particularly when the new direction from the top is in conflict with the current function and flow.

Never make an assumption about the way in which the operations process *actually* functions. There may be company standard operation procedures (SOPs), but things morph rapidly. If the culture is not explicit about what is required and if a change occurs in the process, then the SOP will not necessarily be updated. I promise you, if you have SOPs and they have not been reviewed in the last twelve months, they will not match how things are really getting done. Check, observe, and listen to how it all works and is interconnected. Then and only then can you know if a new idea, strategy, or tactic will work.

Verify the efficiency and effectiveness of the current function and flow. Unless it has recently been through a period of comprehensive analysis, there is almost always a level of waste in the process. Eliminate what can be eliminated, change what needs to be changed, and then move to the next level of the game.

Ecosystems

Spend the allotted time away from the office and create the strategic plan, create an implementation plan, create a tactical plan, create a communication plan, create a human resource plan, and create all of the other plans. But do not stop there. Test your assumptions with key employees at all levels of the organization and then adjust the detailed implementation plan with specific KPIs.

The term *ecosystem* captures the infinite complexity of nature. An organization's ecosystem captures the limitless possibilities, the interwoven intricacy, and the life and death of a company.

In an organization, we are dealing with a living, breathing entity. Therefore, the strategy is also a living, breathing mechanism. The organization is an ecosystem—a complex and interconnected system. If you move one piece within the system, there will be a related effect somewhere else. Everything has an equal and opposite reaction. For example, according to meteorologist Edward Lorenz, who coined The Butterfly Effect Theory:

> *The Butterfly Effect grants the power to cause a hurricane in China to a butterfly flapping its wings in New Mexico. It may take a very long time, but the connection is real. If the butterfly had not flapped its wings at just the right point in space/time, the hurricane would not have happened.[7]*

Adapt Or Die

According to a much-paraphrased conclusion by Charles Darwin, author of *Origin of the Species*, it is not the strongest species that survive, nor the most intelligent, but the ones most responsive to change. On his journey to the Galapagos, he found cactus that did not have prickly needles; the spines were soft to the touch. When he asked why cactus elsewhere are prickly, he was told it is to stave

---

[7] Shaul, Deborah. *The Business Textbook*. S.l.: Balboa Press, 2017.

off predators. On the Galapagos Islands, no creatures try to eat the cactus.

The corporate lifecycle is a perfect example of how companies or products go through the lifecycle, from start-up to extinction. Adaptation is a huge part of any company, and if companies are not adapting to the changing environment, they can get eaten or die.

Executives must have a single focus on the strategy. Then, every thread of fiber that creates the woven tapestry of the organization should, individually and collectively, focus on driving implementation by changing tactics when barriers arise, or through ongoing monitoring of outcomes. It is important to morph, to change colors, but always to stay true to the organization's identified strategy and who you want to be as you guide the process.

All of the organization's systems in which we work exhibit complex and chaotic behavior. Recognizing the chaotic, fractious nature of our world can give us new insights, power, and wisdom. For example, by understanding the complex, chaotic dynamics of the atmosphere, a balloon pilot can "steer" a balloon to a desired location.

The more closely we link function and flow, the better we can manage the balance of chaos and calm. All organizations are affected by chaos. Chaos theory helps us expect the unexpected and aids in managing the unpredictable. Chaos theory also deals with nonlinear things that are essentially impossible to predict or control, like turbulence, weather, the stock market, our thoughts, and so on. An ecological corporate balance of chaos and calm is essential to survivability.

By understanding that our ecosystems, our social systems, and our economic systems are interconnected, we can hope to avoid actions that may end up being detrimental to our long-term well-being.

Unpredictability

Because we can never know all of the initial conditions of a complex system in sufficient (i.e., perfect) detail, we cannot hope to predict the ultimate fate of a complex system. Even slight errors in measuring the state of a system will be amplified dramatically, rendering any prediction useless. Since it is impossible to measure the effects of all the butterflies (and more unpredictability) in the world, accurate long-range weather prediction will always remain impossible. Those same forces and factors exist in an organization.

Order And Disorder

Chaos does not simply mean disorder. Chaos explores the transitions between order and disorder, which often occur in surprising ways.

ACTIONABLE CONNECTION

1. Assess the function and flow to be sure it is understood and running as planned.

2. Plan for the unpredictable and unexpected by creating awareness of risks and rewards. By realizing that both the unpredictable and unexpected exist and must be factored into your equations, you are ahead of the game.

3. Understand how interconnected the entire organization is by realizing that it is an ecosystem, as complicated and as interconnected as our planet.

4. Adapt to the ever-changing environment or the organization will die.

5. Simplify the flow and function of the work environment by evaluating and reevaluating constantly.

6. Realize that existing profit centers, products, or services may have served their purpose. They may have lived or contributed to their full capacity, and now it is time to make them extinct.

7. Always be open to change and provide opportunities for new growth or new characters to enter the ecosystem to ensure the continued health of the organization.

8. Keep the ecosystem healthy and realize that if it is under stress, the entire ecosystem can collapse.

9. Never forget the forest for the trees and always pick the weeds.

10. Balance chaos with calm.

CHAPTER 10

Failure #8:
Not Properly Preparing
The Executive Team

One guarantee: As a part of a company's many growing pains, the executive team will need to make adjustments. We all need to take a step back and recognize, reflect, and resolve this issue. The executives on your team who got you to where you are may not be the same executives who can get you to where you want to go. People may not have the ability or drive, and we must accept it.

This concept is essential to any business, whether you are the CEO of a publicly traded company or privately held company, whether you as a leader want to continue to run the business in your current capacity or move to a passive, hands-off leadership state of behavior, or whether you want to transition to a founder role, chairperson, work with investors, or straight-out sell.

One thing is sure: You will need to be fearless, make difficult decisions, and get the right people at the table.

If not, it becomes comparable to a prison that has you trapped.

Jim Collins, in his 2009 book *Good to Great*, states:

> *It is better to first get the right people on the bus, the wrong people off the bus, and the right people in the right seats, and then figure out where to drive.*[8]

CEOs often assemble a competent leadership team or inherit a good or bad team. But no matter how the team was assembled, every leader needs to carefully take note of the team's performance. Over time and unintentionally, some CEOs have kept leaders past their ability to perform at the level the business requires. They do not have the right people to handle the current constraints, find and implement new ideas, and lead in a world of uncertainty.

Frequently, many leaders have been compartmentalized in their business units and only see a narrow view of their position and activities. Some people do not have the capacity to move into a strategic position to help scale the business.

Having personnel in the right positions and leveraging their talents can make a significant difference in the speed and efficiency of the strategic implementation process. So why are we leaving executives in positions past their

---

[8] Collins, James C. *Good to Great: Why Some Companies Make the Leap ... and Others Don't.* Collins, 2009.

prime? For me, personally, I believe the number one reason is we have a difficult time articulating weaknesses, then confronting people with lack of performance or skill, and then we do not want them to be angry or disappointed with us.

Our mindset and intention at the core is an understanding that such leaders are not bad people; they just do not have the skills to take it to the next level. Leaders must be aware that some folks have limitations due to lack of experience, lack of breadth and depth of understanding of what is happening outside the work environment, lack of professional development, or lack of personal motivation. In any case, changes may need to be made for the betterment of the organization and for the individual to be personally more successful. I want to emphasize: A lack of fit in an executive's current role does not mean he or she needs to be fired. It just means a better place needs to be found for the executive to personally thrive, thus assisting the organization to thrive.

At the bottom line, there must be a point in time when a leader needs to be courageous and make changes—if you wait too long, each day racks up costs, financially and emotionally.

Here are some thoughts about how to create a superior executive team and all of the right people are in place.

Establish And Enforce High Standards

Affirm your current leadership team is working to meet current needs and identify those who are forward thinkers. Be intentional and honest with yourself by making observations and evaluations: who is really not a right fit anymore? Pay attention to those who are thought partners. Who shows up to the table prepared? Who is always unprepared? Ask yourself who is sharing new insights, articulating opinions that demonstrate forward thinking, and making thoughtful and well-researched suggestions?

If you are not sure, ask individuals to develop a business plan to address future business opportunities. When providing information about the requirements, strike a balance between giving too many parameters to not providing enough requirements. Each person should create a well thought-out concept, complete the research, and prepare a business plan.

I worked with a service company that was in the process of a major transition. It was moving from 100-percent family-ownership to receiving investment funds from a private equity firm. An executive team analysis was completed. We asked each individual to work on a business plan supporting the organizational growth into the future, looking ahead three to five years.

The results: The majority of individuals completed the plan. Out of the group who completed the plan, only two were outstanding. In fact, they were so applicable, the CEO had their authors work on the projects and implement their ideas. The others provided average plans; one was not well developed. Another executive never bothered to complete a plan, stating he was too busy. Three people are no longer a part of that executive team.

Another important reminder: CEOs should hold everyone to the same high standard—do not expect more or allow less from any one team member. Establishing high standards and believing in your team's ability to perform to them is contagious and helps create a results-oriented culture inside your business.

We all want to believe everyone is competent and integral to the organization. Nonetheless, believing in their ability to deliver is not always enough. And not everyone is as integral to the organization as often we imagine. In fact, hesitation to let low performers go is really fear: We know if a key person exits, we don't really comprehend everything they do, and then it feels as if we will need to cover that person's work. Who needs more work on their plate? Because of these thoughts, often, executives make excuses for friends and family who started in the trenches with them when they founded a company, or in an early executive position. I would ask, are you holding everyone to the same standard? Or do you allow yourself to make excuses?

Grace Under Pressure Is An Executive Quality

Another opportunity is to observe how people act under pressure and when the stakes are high. Often, we appraise people when business is good, time is available in abundance, and we are going about normal daily operations. But most people can perform well under these circumstances. The real test is when things are not going well. How do they handle risk? Do they always hold back on thoughtful opinions and new ideas for fear of rejection? Do they get flustered, live in the negative, or use passive-aggressive language?

I have seen unprofessional behavior. There are two specific situations I can recall in which executives did not handle the pressure well.

In the first situation, I was sequestered in a dark, dingy conference room with the executive team. Tensions were high as we were discussing (well, maybe debating) a financial crisis. During a brainstorming session, Executive A inquisitively asked Executive B if he could figure out a way to reduce one full-time employee. With no warning, Executive B stood up, yelled, chucked papers all the way across the table, and walked out. I guess that meant "No."

Unfortunately, this behavior was commonplace, and the CEO made no effort to correct the behavior. The CEO continued to make excuses for him, stating, "We need him because he knows so much and has a longstanding history with the company." The cumulative impact of the CEO not taking action and Executive B continuing this behavior caused issues, including how others responded to the circumstance. The results of both their behavior resulted in a downward spiral of team morale; other intelligent, key executives left the organization.

The second was a shock-and-awe situation. Imagine months and months of people working together to develop and roll out an entirely new strategic plan. Many large and small group meetings had been held to discuss ideas and concepts; the staff was eager and energized by the engagement. Staff mentioned how they finally felt like this was the new beginning they had been craving for a long time.

The big day came. Everyone—all the staff and senior leaders—gathered in a big room that was decorated. Candy was at the center of each table. The meeting started out with a round robin of introductions and people taking the opportunity to share how they had played a part in the planning. Then, the CEO officially began the meeting by sharing his journey to the role of CEO and why the strategic work was so important. People were enthralled with his story. After his story, he began to share the well-developed PowerPoint that showed everyone the final strategic operational execution plan.

But what happened next was incredibly discouraging. A quarter of the way through the meeting, the CEO respectfully asked the group if they had any questions. One employee asked a question that addressed a sensitive topic about resources. The employee's boss whipped his head around, interrupted and angrily said, that is not a discussion for the group. The CEO politely reacted by saying, "It is OK, I am fine with the question."

The employee then asked the CEO a clarifying question. His boss once again interrupted, defended himself, blamed the employee, and then literally stormed out of the room. Everyone in the room, including the CEO, was visibly stunned. Wow, that was tough to recover from. Unfortunately, after further investigation, it was discovered this was the manager's modus operandi. Shortly thereafter, he resigned.

Hire For Cultural Fit

Next concept: a team member needs to be selected to fit into the present culture with the ability and interest to transition into the culture of the future. As many organizations shift and grow, the culture needs to be highly managed. If a team member does not fit in, this could cause a great deal of false strategic execution starts. "Culture eats strategy for breakfast" is a famous quotation attributed to the late business management guru Peter Drucker.

Let us talk about the hiring process. All team members should be hired for where you are going, not where you are currently in the company growth cycle. I know this is easier said than done, as I faced many barriers to hiring the right team members. One of those barriers is often the human resources (HR) department, which has been relegated to the tactical duty of reading a job description and filling it with a person who meets the minimum requirements.

I recommend we figure out how to develop our HR leaders to be strategic and have them reevaluate the hiring process. A good place to start is developing job descriptions that address future requirements. We should stop using the typical, boring words that address tactical skills and only address the requirements of the current job. We need to develop job descriptions that address the future state of the organization.

When hiring for the right fit, we need to understand and state behaviors regarding what is required, what the right fit looks like, and what it takes to work within the organization's culture. An executive needs to know where the industry is going and how the executive can be a thought partner—why shouldn't the top executive candidates be subject to the same grueling process, writing a business plan as a test for fit?

In summary, the more successful and complicated the business becomes, the more you need to look further into the future versus managing day-to-day operations. To do this, it is imperative you have the right people at the table, at the right time, so they can help you get to where you are going.

ACTIONABLE TRANSFORMATION

1. Analyze your current team and recognize those executives who do not have the ability or drive to move into the future.

2. Prepare to take courageous action to improve your executive team.

3. Develop ways to observe and manage the team's performance on an ongoing basis.

4. Be aware that most leaders become compartmentalized in their business units and therefore may need to develop and expand their abilities.

5. Stay aware of and leverage each person's talents and observe those who take on assignments with a new perspective.

6. Be clear on your vision and expectations, so it is easier to hold everyone to the same high standards.

7. Observe how people act under pressure.

8. Make decisions quickly.

9. Observe your actions toward those executives or family members who have been with the company for a while—be sure you understand their capabilities without adding emotions to the analysis.

10. Understand your current culture and the future culture in an effort to place everyone in the right role, including new hires.

PART III

Beyond Better Implementation

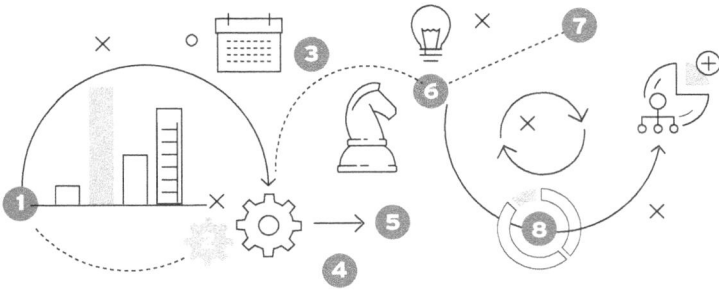

CHAPTER 11

....

Sustaining A Success Culture

Successfully implementing a strategy is most certainly the desire of all CEOs and business owners. A foundation must be set, and this is accomplished by defining the organization's culture. Without a solid culture, attempts to implement strategy will likely be doomed.

What is your organizational culture? Is it well defined and integrated into your strategy and implementation plan?

On the face of it, organizational culture has been described as the company norms, practices, and values as set forth by the founder and leaders. People may say "It is just the way we do things around here." Many organizations have attempted strategy planning and implementation without totally understanding the intricacy of the culture and how it can affect implementation. It is important to be aware of and identify how the integration of cultural concepts and behaviors are a part of all strategic planning phases.

A part of the problem is we tend to use the word "things" to describe culture; no one really has in-depth knowledge of the *behaviors* associated with "things." A more comprehensive definition of culture will be critical for success.

Why? Because culture is an enterprise-wide proposition and should be the strategic anchor. I know you know that building, revitalizing, or changing a culture is easier said than done. Do you first need to define the culture before the strategy, or complete the strategy to define and refine the culture? No matter which option you decide, to successfully implement your desired strategy, you must find ways to sustain a high-performance success culture.

Here are a few things to be discerning about to assist you in achieving a culture of success, and to keep you ahead of your competition.

High-Performance Leaders

Leaders are the living embodiment of what a successful culture is like in action. How one interacts inside and outside the boardroom has an impact on the way people respond.

Leaders who successfully implement strategy help drive the understanding of behaviors that are required within the culture of the organization. They are honest, provide feedback, and openly receive feedback. They consciously embody the behaviors they require in others without pretense and arrogance.

Leaders should have a presence when they walk into a room: confident, aware of those who are in the room, and open about your intentions. Your body language tells a lot about you before you even say one word.

External Focus

One often creates an unrealistic strategy with unrealistic goals by not being keen to the external forces. Culture and strategy go hand in hand, and at the most basic level, both are a set of choices and trade-offs about setting a set of criteria for success regarding where the organization will compete, invest, and win.

To ensure a success culture, one must keep an eye on external events and conditions. Often, leaders get caught in the insularity of the demands of their position. Many focus on internal issues—the day-to-day—causing them to lose sight of the external environment. When this happens, competitors can take them by surprise. Customers will leave.

Do you remember Blockbuster? Borders? Toys "R" Us? I believe we are in for many more disrupters. For example, we are not done seeing the disruption caused by the rideshare business in either the transportation or the car manufacturing industries.

When there is a lack of external focus, competitors may develop a similar product that satisfies your customers' needs and at a lower cost. Technology innovation can jump your competitor ahead; your processes may become outdated. Sometimes competitive technology is so advanced and cheaper, you will not be able to catch up.

In addition, with rapid technology and innovation advances by competitors, your employees might move on to another company that promises them more tech opportunities, innovative advances, and a flexible culture. When they leave your organization, they are taking knowledge with them. I suspect we don't even know the amount of knowledge they are taking with them—right into the hands of competitors.

People As Assets

Success cultures view people as assets to be encouraged and inspired.

Most leaders put their people in the liability column emotionally, constantly analyzing the payroll line—which for most businesses, understandably, is the biggest expense. This evaluation through the single lens of finance—assets versus liabilities, as it is on the financial statements—translates into treating people like a liability, which causes us in turn to make low-level and quick decisions versus high-performing, strategic decisions. Looking at people as a quick way to cut costs creates a cultural attitude of people as expendable. On the flip side, building a culture of people as assets creates more enthusiasm to do what is right for the entire organizational ecosystem, creating a strategy that has some teeth to build an engaged workforce.

Another important aspect of people as an asset is preparing them to do superior work. Investing in your people through basic training does *not* work. Experiential and real-world training and knowledge sharing, on the other hand, builds a competitive workforce and collaborative workforce. Creating learning modules in brief simulations that are informative with real-time applicability makes for a more engaged and efficient workforce.

Emotions

Change the narrative and balance between the right-brain and left-brain thinking—analytical versus emotional—versus only emphasizing the right brain.

Most people are uncomfortable dealing with emotions in a business setting. In fact, for decades, we were taught to show no emotions, but rather to be stoic as leaders. With changes in the workforce demographics, however, the speed with which changes are happening, and with the political landscape, in order to create an implementation culture, we must be in tune with emotional experiences. We need to consider all stakeholder groups inside and outside the organization, including employees, customers, communities, and investors. Sometimes even the emotions of members of our employees' families need to be taken into consideration.

As leaders, we need to accept the fact that the fate of our best-laid plans depends on the emotional intelligence of these groups. We are great at working every plan through the right-brain, but we need to incorporate the left-brain—the driver of emotions.

In 2010, Daniel Goleman wrote the book, *Emotional Intelligence: Why It Can Matter More Than IQ.*[9] In the book, he states, "The emotional brain responds to an event more quickly than the thinking brain." Yet we continually try to logically convince employees to follow along, instead of working toward the emotional *why* and WIIFM.

If we become more attuned and receptive to subtle nonverbal signs of stakeholder emotions, we as leaders are more likely to gain the credibility that is required for a success culture. Bottom line: Emotionally illiterate leadership will give rise to an impotent and change-averse culture.

It is inevitable you will be faced with addressing stakeholders' emotions, so either do it up front and throughout the process or deal with it later, when it is out of control and unreasonable emotions are being presented.

---

[9] Goleman, Daniel. *Emotional Intelligence: Why It Can Matter More than IQ.* London: Bloomsbury, 2010.

Right-Size The Organization

The organizational structure, design, and size follow strategy, and leaders strive to find the optimal balance.

Have you ever tried to put a square peg in a round hole? You can do it, but you have to beat the heck out of the peg, and there is a lot of destruction. Still, it can be a fast process.

This goes back to the conversation about creating the right resources, processes, and getting the right positions and people in place for future growth. Let's stop trying to create amazing strategies that will not fit your organization. Figure out what needs to be changed by looking at the following:

- **The plans:** What is your strategy and implementation plan and how does your current culture help or hinder the right-sizing of the organization?

- **The people:** Align everyone's goals with organizational objectives according to the future of the organization within the new or redefined culture.

- **Process:** Align processes with objectives, expectations, metrics, and performance to the strategy and create a culture of collaboration and appreciation.

- **Profit:** Optimize core products and services and then assess cultural fit, the function of the organization, and feasibility.

- **Perspective:** Find a point of view for your culture of success. Know where you are in the sea of competitors as well as the trend. Manage others' perspectives and help them see the wisdom of alternative viewpoints in an effort to create a success culture that aligns with the strategy.

Action, Not Perfection

If we move away from action and into perfection, the culture will be stunted by analysis paralysis.

Most organizations will analyze the good, bad, and really ugly mistakes to figure out what went wrong. But the difference between a second-rate company and a remarkable company is its reaction to a mistake.

Is there a collective learning, or a continued rumination on the blunder? Ruminating causes the workforce to become paralyzed for fear of making another mistake and reaping punishment. Successful cultures embrace mistakes, learn, grow, and move on.

Successful cultures figure out what went wrong and make a course correction rather than abandoning a plan completely in a fit of frustration, panic, and embarrassment. This emotional abandonment is what causes culture and strategy to be perceived as the "flavor of the month." It is important for building a successful culture and implementation plan to empower employees to collaborate, not compete, and to tackle problems with confidence, not a sense of failure (or "I am going to get in trouble").

Competitive Context

The competitive context is the factor which most strongly influences strategy (and by default, influences culture development).

Given today's economic environment, competitiveness, and rapid diffusion of technology, maintaining a vibrant and distinctive culture may be one of the few areas left where leaders can generate long-term competitive advantage.

Politically Savvy

First, get rid of the politics mentality, which really translates into thinking about the needs of the entire organization versus the needs of the self.

It is best to build a transparent culture by having overt dialogue instead of allowing for covert (secret) conversations. When concealed conversations are the norm, issues will not be raised openly, and you will not know how to make adjustments to the implementation of the organizational strategy.

Make it easy to be the bearer of bad news by eliminating the fear that causes inaction. Welcoming bad news from all levels of the organization converts into good news for building a success culture and the ability to implement the strategy.

By eliminating the politics first, leaders establish a culture in which people are willing to share information among and between departments. The opposite happens when a competitive environment is created and information hoarding becomes prevalent.

Focus On Strengths

Focusing on strengths builds a positive, engaged workforce. In an organization that constantly focuses on weaknesses—which is both dehumanizing and demoralizing—people do not respond to being berated, either implicitly or explicitly. This may not be you, but ask yourself, who is working under these old laws of leadership?

As stated earlier, Jim Collins taught us to get the right people on the bus in the right seats in his book *Good to Great*. Basically, it is about finding strengths, leveraging those strengths, and further developing those strengths.

A successful culture means that leaders know what strengths are required for strategic implementation. Leaders are not afraid of identifying those strengths and analyzing the current workforce according to the needs and then taking action to make changes in the structure and makeup of the workforce. Again, that might mean people shift their roles or move on to another opportunity.

In summary, to successfully execute on strategy, a solid strategic plan, active planning, solid leadership, awareness of emotions, and an even better success culture are required.

CHAPTER 12

•••

The Beginning: A Process, Not A Project

So there you have it; the eight ways great strategies fail and how to fix them.

Did any of these ring true for you?

My hope is that this information helps you ignite a movement for implementation success throughout your organization, along with creating a work environment where people like to come to work each day. This journey is a *process* of interactions and exchanges, not a short-term *project* that is not integrated into your corporate ecosystem.

Here are my last few words of advice (at least within the confines of this book). Please do not focus on the mistake side of the column but on the success column. As mentioned in chapter 11, focusing on the strengths of the organization and the people creates greater impact than focusing on weaknesses.

Above all, explain what is meant by strategy, implementation, and the WIIFM. Cascade objectives from the strategic retreat to the strategic implementation retreat to the people, thus creating real outcomes with real work—and the *right* work. Do not uncouple completely from the idea of a focused strategy, but be agile with the tactics to meet the strategic objectives.

Be sure you:

- **Connect the mission to the strategy.** Connect everything you do to the core of the organization—the mission, vision, values, and culture. These key metrics are the guiding star to navigate the strategy.

- **Pull input from the top and bottom of the organization.** Move beyond your competitors and eliminate the need to push everything downward from the top. Create opportunities for inclusivity from all stakeholders in the organization and expect people to be engaged in the execution. Pull input from the bottom up.

- **Understand the real meaning of strategy.** Become a champion of explaining the real meaning of strategy and the implementation requirements throughout the organization. Be clear in the definition as it relates to requirements for success.

- **Focus on the critical few.** Be hypervigilant about finding the key, critical, few players who can drive for strategic results. Let the rest be tactical executors.

- **Maintain focused momentum.** Construct opportunities for building and sustaining momentum by defining priorities, success measurements, and the roles everyone plays in the execution of the strategy.

- **Seize the right resources.** Identify, acquire, and allocate a well-rounded cache of resources. Focus on the high-yield priorities—then let go of the rest.

- **Align to function and flow.** Ruthlessly link all people, processes, outcomes, and resources to the function and flow of the operations, so the right work gets done.

- **Prepare the executive team.** Assess who is prepared and dedicated to the strategic execution mindset and has the skills to execute. Then invest in their success.

Finally, give your people the benefit of the doubt. Remember, people want to be part of something extraordinary, and they want to follow leaders who provide a clear vision for the future.

Provide the right strategy, the right tactics, and the right measurements, and you will see your business and your people grow exponentially.

APPENDIX A

....

Acknowledgments

To my Mom and Pops, the consummate supporters of all my endeavors.

Mom, you have always been the positive voice—my number one supporter—through all of the ups and downs. You never lost faith in my abilities and dreams. Pops, an exemplary person who took me under your wing and into your heart from the beginning of courting my Mom—thank goodness you won over Mom—we love having you in our family. Pops, you are a well-respected serial entrepreneur who has generously helped so many other entrepreneurs get their start. You are the one who encouraged me to go out on my own, do what I do best, and then supported my undertaking in writing this book. Mom and Pops, you are my heroes, and I will be ever grateful to both of you.

To Cambria, my beloved partner and absolute enthusiast. Without your generosity, encouragement, and insights, this would have taken many more hours, days, and even months to materialize. I thank you for our in-depth dialogue about business issues that are present in any organization, the deliberation over the correct use of the written and spoken word, and of course, deciding on the next vacation—work/life balance.

To Henry DeVries, CEO of Indie Books International, my amazing editor. Henry, thank you for accepting me as a client. Your extraordinary use of the English language was instrumental to the success of this book. You were able to help me articulate my message and put my ideas into words. You went above and beyond your editing role—you helped drive me, create a plan for the execution of this book, and you are just an all-around big-hearted person.

A thank-you to all of my National Association of Women Business Owners (NAWBO): some of you are my collaborators, some of you are my clients, and most importantly, some of you are my friends and golf cronies. It has been a pleasure getting to know many of you and serving you at the local Orange County chapter and for NAWBO California. Thank you for supporting my book journey.

APPENDIX B

•••

About the Author

Dr. Theresa Ashby is known as a stratologist. She is recognized as a savvy, provocative and genuine individual and is widely respected for her business acumen. Theresa is a national business and success consultant, advisor, and speaker who is passionate about driving businesses forward, as this is the *only* thing she believes helps grow the economy on all levels.

When she is on stage educating and entertaining the audience, she works to capture hearts while driving home lessons that can be implemented immediately. Her ability to lead and develop people and to unite teams around a common vision has been paramount to her success throughout her career. Theresa impacts organizations through delivery of groundbreaking operational implementation strategies, processes, and advisement. Her background includes thirty years of experience in a variety of leadership roles, managing a $50 million budget, overseeing $1.7 billion of capital improvements, running hundreds of teams at one time, implementing operational strategies, and serving as VP of operations for a leading healthcare organization.

She currently is the CEO of Strategic Implementation Solutions, assistant professor at Loma Linda University, serves as the vice president for the National Association of Women Business Owners-California, holds a seat on a corporate board, and enjoys traveling the world.

APPENDIX C

··

Resources From Strategic Implementation Solutions

STRATEGY OPTIMIZED • TALENT ENERGIZED • VISION REALIZED

We provide strategic execution consulting and advisement for founders, entrepreneurs, executives, and investors working in and with micro to midmarket companies. Our goal is to help our clients achieve:

- *More engagement from their people across the company continuum*

- *More focus on profit center management*

- *More alignment on productivity and outcomes*

- *More systematized operations and processes*

- *More peace of mind*

These allow for an improved return on investment on their time and their resources.

We help our clients increase value through an integrated approach to strategy execution, ensuring the company is focused on process, people, and profit.

To contact Dr. Theresa M. Ashby, CEO of Strategic Implementation Solutions, for a speaking or consulting engagement, please call 949-533-8832.

APPENDIX D

Works Referenced

Collins, James C. *Good to Great: Why Some Companies Make the Leap ... and Others Don't.* Collins, 2009.

Goleman, Daniel. *Emotional Intelligence: Why It Can Matter More than IQ.* London: Bloomsbury, 2010.

"Gravity Hill." *Wikipedia,* https://en.wikipedia.org/wiki/Gravity_hill. Accessed.

"Nano-Cap". Investopedia.com. Reviewed by James Chen. November 16, 2017. Accessed November 19, 2019. https://investinganswers.com/financial-dictionary/stock-market/nano-caps-602

Shaul, Deborah. *Business Textbook.* Balboa Press, 2017.

Sull, Donald, Rebecca Homkes, and Charles Sull. "Why Strategy Execution Unravels—and What to Do About It." *Harvard Business Review,* March 2015.

Sundheim, Doug. "3 Reasons Your Strategy Meetings Irritate Your Team." *Harvard Business Review*, March 1, 2016. Accessed November 19, 2019. https://hbr.org/2016/03/3-reasons-your-strategy-meetings-irritate-your-team